Group Games
Emotional Strength & Self-Esteem

ROSEMARIE PORTMANN

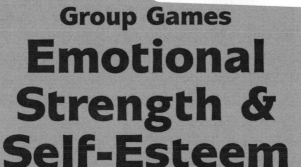

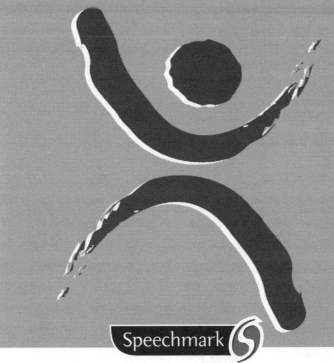

Speechmark

Speechmark Publishing Ltd
Telford Road • Bicester • Oxon OX26 4LQ • United Kingdom

Originally published in German by Don Bosco Verlag, München under the title *Spiele, die stark machen*, © Don Bosco Verlag, München 1998

Published by
Speechmark Publishing Ltd, Telford Road, Bicester, Oxon OX26 4LQ, UK
www.speechmark.net

© Speechmark Publishing Ltd, 2002

First published 2002
Reprinted 2003, 2004, 2005, 2006

All rights reserved. The whole of this work, including all text and illustrations, is protected by copyright. No parts of this work may be loaded, stored, manipulated, reproduced, or transmitted in any form or by any means, electronic or mechanical, including photocopying and recording, or by any information, storage and retrieval system without prior written permission from the publisher, on behalf of the copyright owner.

002-5109/Printed in the United Kingdom/1010

British Library Cataloguing in Publication Data

Portmann, Rosemarie
Emotional strength & self-esteem. – (Group Games)
1. Self-esteem in children   2. Group games
I. Title
155.4'182'5

ISBN 0 86388 394 X
ISBN 978 0 86388 394 1

Contents

About the Author

Rosemarie Portmann Dip (Psychol) is manager of the educational psychology service for the local education authority in Wiesbaden, Germany. She is also an adviser to the Parents Association in Hessen.

Rosemarie is a lecturer at the Institute for Educational Pedagogy and Teaching Methods in the Elementary and Primary Department of the University of Frankfurt.

She is the author of several successful games books and other specialist publications, including *Relaxation & Concentration* and *Dealing with Aggression*, which are both in Speechmark's 'Group Games' series.

Acknowledgement

Thank you to Lilo Seelos, the translator.

Games

Gaining Strength – Showing Strength 69

Introduction

TRUE STRENGTH: DEALING SUCCESSFULLY WITH YOURSELF AND OTHERS

Why do we need games that help develop strength? Are people not strong and powerful enough already? Is it not one of the main problems in today's society that children and teenagers, as well as adults, utilise their strength and power without consideration for others? Should we not try to dampen rather than strengthen the self-confidence of most people? Unfortunately, we are too easily deceived by cause and effect, and take what we perceive and experience as everyday reality.

In fact, many people have too little, rather than too much, self-confidence. They are unsure of their self-worth and do not think themselves capable of very much. They have learned that, frequently, they are not good enough, and therefore feel that they have to work continuously at proving themselves. Self-confidence and self-esteem are not God-given. They are qualities that develop gradually starting in early childhood. Children who, from the very beginning, are encouraged to develop self-esteem, who are loved unconditionally, who are thought to be capable of doing things, and who experience recognition and acknowledgement, will grow up into strong and self-confident individuals. But disappointment and emotional wounding are likely to dampen, or even destroy, any self-confidence and self-esteem in the course of time.

Everybody wants to be strong and self-confident and be acknowledged and recognised by others. Self-esteem and self-confidence are essential for the development of a strong personality. An awareness of our own strength and worth – and, of course, our own limits – generates optimism and inner strength, which enable us to achieve our potential and develop into the person that we could actually be. Self-confident people feel that they are able to influence their environment. They realise that they can actively affect things, rather than simply having to react passively to things that they are confronted with by the outside world. Because of this, self-confident children and teenagers are more likely to explore future perspectives than less self-confident ones. They view life more positively, and are always prepared to embrace new experiences. Failure and setbacks are perceived as learning experiences and do not discourage them from looking ahead and trying again. Criticism is accepted, and not considered to be an attack on their feelings of self-worth.

Strong and self-confident people also benefit the wider community. Only those people who are happy to accept and enjoy themselves, and who are at peace with themselves, have the ability to live peacefully with others, to accept and support others. Self-confident and self-assured people are able to stand up and assert themselves. They can communicate their visions and wishes in an appropriate manner without pressurising others or exercising power.

In many people, a lack of self-confidence is closely related to fears and uncertainties and to a feeling of being neglected.

Frequently these feelings prevent people from discovering their own inner resources and utilising them effectively. Interactive situations are often perceived as a threat. When some people feel threatened it can trigger aggression and violence which in itself is a mask for feelings of inferiority and fear. Someone who tries to frighten others is generally frightened themselves, and not really particularly strong.

A person whose self-esteem is dependent on the judgement of others is also in danger of being put down and exploited. People with little self-confidence not only become culprits, they also become victims. Their behaviour can cause dislike and provoke aggression.

Unfortunately, our educational and social system still produces more unconfident than confident people. Children are looked upon as future adults, but are not considered as equals when they are children. Often they are not thought of as being capable of doing much. They are more likely to be criticised or punished than to be strengthened and praised. Children and teenagers are often criticised when they try to articulate their needs or ask for their rights to be met. Generally, they are not brought up to express their interests appropriately, and to recognise and reject the inappropriate demands of others. Self-denial is fostered in preference to self-assertion. Educators therefore have a special responsibility to help children and teenagers develop self-confidence and self-assurance.

The games suggested in this book are meant to provide ideas for those working with children, adolescents and adults to:

◆ Highlight human strengths and power as a central theme
◆ Help them discover their own strengths and weaknesses
◆ Help them learn how to gain inner strength and act with confidence
◆ Learn how to be assertive while living respectfully with others.

GAMES AND ACTIVITIES AS A MEANS OF TEACHING

Group games and activities are an easy way of initiating the learning processes. They offer open and interactive systems that allow participants to experience themselves and others in a variety of settings. Participants can contribute their feelings and needs to the situation, can become active themselves, and can experience the consequences of their actions without fear. Interactive games aimed at building self-confidence require participants to put themselves in situations that, for them, tend to be associated with uncertainty. The game format of the activities eases these feelings of uncertainty, fear and threat as everyday situations are restructured in a socially controlled way, in a less complex manner with action and interaction being facilitated by a limitation of behaviour possibilities.

Games in a group setting create a basis for topical discussion where everybody starts out from the same point and then has the benefit of shared experiences. This is quite different to learning from, say, use of a presentation or a film as the games themselves are an active learning experience.

While the games and exercises presented in this book represent group activities, they nevertheless tap into the individuality and varying abilities of the group members. Participants are put into situations that allow them to:

◆ Gain a better understanding of their own possibilities, abilities and desires
◆ Develop their self-assurance, and express their desires, interests and intentions in a clear and non-threatening manner
◆ Practise asserting themselves appropriately within a group setting
◆ Through the use of creative methods, experience a feeling of emotional well-being and enjoyment in an accepting social context.

Successful participation in individual activities facilitates a momentary increase in self-esteem and, as a result, self-confidence. Obviously, one-off participation in any of the activities presented cannot be expected to permanently rectify a serious lack of self-confidence and self-esteem. However, the situations experienced during the activities are important steps towards this, especially if they are continually repeated and reinforced.

Using the activities

This book contains 111 games and exercises that have been tested and proved in practice. They have been carefully selected with the aim of highlighting as many different possibilities for integral learning as possible.

Details such as age appropriateness and possibilities for variation have deliberately been omitted. The content and rules of the majority of games and exercises can be adapted without any problems for children, adolescents and adults depending on needs and abilities. In order for the games and exercises to achieve their desired learning outcome, they can be easily tailored to the particular needs of a group and its individual members.

The games and exercises in this book generally do not require special preparation and the majority of activities can be carried out without any materials. A few require simple everyday objects, which are listed at the beginning of the activity description.

A prerequisite for the success of the games and exercises is the endeavour to create an atmosphere of trust within the group. Nevertheless, it is possible that individual group members may not wish to join in. If that is the case, they should not be pressurised into participating. Generally, they are likely to gain trust by watching the activities from the periphery, and will approach the activities gradually until they do finally join in. In most cases, disruptions due to group members who are very low in self-esteem tend to cease after a period of settling in.

Experience has shown that, in the end, everybody tends to enjoy the games and activities.

After every exercise or game there needs to be some time for evaluation. Participants need an opportunity to express the experiences and feelings they had during the activities.

Trainers wanting to use the games and exercises in this book do not require specific competencies except one: they should themselves enjoy participating in group activities. Apart from this, they ought to have tried any activity themselves, ideally together with others, before they offer it to a group. The development of self-assurance and self-confidence with the help of games and exercises necessitates self-assured and self-confident trainers and facilitators. Successful application of the activities requires trainers who have asked themselves the following questions: How do I rate myself in relation to the topic? What could I do and what may I need to do, in order to sense and reflect more self-esteem?

Games &
Exercises for
Emotional
Strength &
Self-Esteem

Strength – What's That?

Today's society, with its increase in individual freedom and the simultaneous loss of a uniform value system, has, for many people, brought with it feelings of uncertainty with regard to ways of helping children and teenagers to grow up into successful people who are able to live harmoniously with each other. Frequently, adults can be heard complaining about the increasing selfishness and lack of consideration among today's youth. The emphasis put on 'I virtues' such as self-realisation, courage and an ability to achieve do not appear to be in balance any more, when compared to the emphasis put on 'us virtues' such as solidarity, group responsibility, consideration for others, ability to compromise and helpfulness.

Often, existing opportunities for individual development are simply discussed pessimistically under the head of egotistical self-realisation. However, individual development can also be viewed optimistically, and can be experienced as an enrichment because it also comprises an opportunity for new understanding of the essential values of personal responsibility. Concepts of duty and acceptance, as well as the concept of self-realisation, can be viewed as something positive and can be linked with each other.

Inner strength proves itself not only in the ability to be at ease with oneself, but also in the ability to know how to handle others in a socially competent manner. All efforts to create 'strong' people therefore have to be based on a reflection of the meaning of one's own strength and the responsibility associated with that strength. The following games and exercises are offered as a gateway to this reflection.

1) The ABC of Power

A handout containing the letters of the alphabet can stimulate individual ideas related to the topic of power and strength. Every group member is given a handout and is asked to write down a 'powerful' word, a 'powerful' sentence or a 'powerful' idea; for example:

A	active	N	nerve
B	Big Brother	O	overpowering
C	control	P	president
D	dynamic	Q	queen
E	energy	R	robust
F	force	S	successful
G	giant	T	tough
H	high-powered	U	Mr Universe
I	influential	V	vigour
J	justice	W	wearing the trousers
K	king	X	strong as an ox
L	leadership	Y	youth of today
M	macho man	Z	zap

Individual ideas for each letter are then written on a big sheet of paper. This way, a wealth of terms and ideas are gathered that describe group members' perceptions of strength and power and provide the group with a lead-in to discussion.

2 **Feeling Strong is Like …**

The construction of metaphors using the sentence beginning 'Feeling strong is like …' offers a good way of introducing the topic area of self-confidence and self-assertion. The impulse words are written in large letters on a flipchart. Group members are asked to write their ideas on strips of card or paper, which are then stuck to the flipchart. For example, Feeling strong is like:

◆ Standing on top of a mountain
◆ Looking down on everybody from the cabin of a truck
◆ Riding really high waves.

What sort of wishes, needs and fantasies can be recognised in these examples? Does 'feeling strong' mean the same as 'feeling superior'? Or is it possible to feel strong without dominating others?

3) A Strong Object

Bring in a box full of small everyday objects. These could include a ball, a stone, a ballpoint pen, a book, a ruler and so on. There have to be at least as many objects as there are group members. There can be more than one of each object.

Every group member chooses one object, which for them symbolises strength. Group members then take it in turns to introduce their object to the group, and provide a reason for their choice. For example:

- ◆ Book: 'For me strength means predominantly mental strength, that's why I chose the small book.'
- ◆ Ball: 'Strength proves itself in the flexibility and agility of a person.'
- ◆ Ruler: 'The ruler reminds me of a stick. I associate strength with hitting.'

An alternative to bringing in objects is to ask participants to choose an object in the room that represents strength.

This exercise is a good way of introducing the topic of strength/power.

4 Picture Puzzle

For this exercise you require pictures (for example, postcards or magazine pictures) that could trigger associations with 'being strong'. Such pictures could be representations of events or people, but also of landscapes and objects. The less concrete they are, the more they are likely to appeal to people's imagination. There should be twice as many pictures as there are participants, to allow an element of choice.

Every group member is asked to select 'their' picture – a picture that they feel best expresses their idea of strength. It does not matter if more than one person chooses the same picture.

In a discussion, group members then explore the following questions: Why did they choose a particular picture? What was it that for them expressed strength/power? Are there similarities among participants with regard to what represents strength and power? What are they?

5 Word Chains

For this game you will need some index cards or small pieces of paper. Group members are asked to build word chains: every word has to start with the last letter of the previous word, and words also have to have some association with strength or power. For example:

courage – energy – youth – headmaster – ruling – …

Words are not just spoken, but are written down individually and then stuck on a board or wall-chart. The game is over when no one can think of another word.

After the game is finished, the words are used to reflect on the topic of strength/power. What do group members associate with strength/power?

6   Drawing Postcards

Every group member is given a blank index card the size of a postcard. They are asked to draw a picture, a sketch, a symbol, a speech bubble with text, and so on, that reflects their perception of strength. The 'postcards' are introduced to the group and discussed.

What ideas have been represented? Are there different views of what represents strength among group members? What are they?

7 Lucky Dip

This game requires a little preparation. Words or terms that bear any relation to the topic 'strength' are written on to many small pieces of paper. The pieces of paper are collected into a bowl or box to make a 'lucky dip'. Group members then take it in turns to draw a piece of paper and decide whether, in their view, the content has anything to do with strength, or not. The pieces of paper are sorted accordingly and posted on to two wall-posters. Once the lucky dip is ended, and all pieces of paper have been sorted into one of the two categories, the two wall-posters are read and discussed. Does everybody agree with the categorisations? Are there different views among group members of what strength is? What are they?

8 Three Powerful Corners

Posters with the following statements are put up in three corners of the room:

1 A truly strong person is never weak

2 A truly strong person never shows their weaknesses

3 A truly strong person can afford to show weaknesses

The group members are encouraged to choose the statement that most reflects their opinion; to walk to the relevant corner; to discuss the statement with other members in that corner, and to come up with reasons and examples to support 'their' argument. Each 'corner' determines a speaker who then represents the group in a plenary discussion.

How did the discussion go? What sort of reasons were given to support the different statements? Did one argument win through? Which one? And why?

9 Powerful Ending

The group leader begins to tell or read a story. The task of the group members is to find a 'powerful' ending to the story. Particularly suitable for this exercise are so-called 'dilemma stories', where two aims fall into conflict with each other. For example:

A girl has been looking forward for some time to going to her best friend's birthday party. Then the girl's mother asks her to baby-sit her little brother, because she has been asked to stand in for someone at work at short notice ...

A boy has a crush on a particular girl. He has invited her to join him and his group when they go clubbing on Saturday night. Then he hears the group leader make derogatory remarks about the girl ...

A teenager has saved up for his first car. He has finally got enough to buy a small second-hand one. Then he finds out that a friend has fallen seriously ill and requires medical treatment that is not easily available in this country and will need paying for ...

The completed stories are read out in a group setting, although no one should be forced to read their story. How difficult was it to come up with a story ending? What sort of endings were found? Which ones are particularly powerful? Why?

10) Give and Take

Bring in a number of small items, but not enough for all group members. Such items could be pencils, balloons, sweets, fruit, and so on.

The group members are given the task of sharing out the items together. They have to ensure that no one is disadvantaged or is feeling disadvantaged. What sort of 'powerful' solution can the group come up with?

(11) Round Story

Ideas of strength and self-confidence can also become clear when writing 'round stories'. The group members are asked to sit in a circle. They have to agree on a topic they are going to write a story about: for example, 'Mrs Smith is thinking powerful thoughts' or 'John the Strong'.

Each group member requires an A4 piece of paper and a pen, and initially has to write down the title and the first two sentences of the story. Then they fold back the paper so that it covers the first sentence, with the second sentence still visible. Papers are then passed on one place to the left, and again each group member writes two sentences that continue the story on their piece of paper, folds over the paper so that only the last sentence can be read, and so on. Whoever gets a piece of paper last in the round writes down a finishing sentence as their second sentence. The story is then finished. Each story should now be back with the person who started it. Stories are 'rolled out' and read aloud.

What was it like to write a story 'blindly'? Difficult, exciting, or simply funny? How well have the 'round stories' worked out? Did everybody stick to the topic? What was said about the topic?

Powerful Poems

Headings related to the topic 'being strong' are cut out randomly from newspapers and magazines. The group is split into sub-groups of four to five members who have to create a 'powerful' poem using the headings or parts of the headings by sequencing them and sticking them on to a piece of paper. The different poems are then posted and commented on by the whole group. For example:

> *Rebels stripped and humiliated officers*
> *Frog-marched through jungle*
> *Protest*
> *The most powerful feature is the price*
> *Choice*
> *Cambridge: Tolerant and serious*
> *A one-woman opposition*
> *Victory over the Kurds*
> *Panic ends as 'ebola' is case of yellow fever*
> *Byers to retain reserve power*
> *Persil powers Unilever*
> *Profits rise*
> *Dutch win at last*
> *Monty in control*
> *Wallace strikes fear in hearts*
> *The boy's done good*

(All headings were taken from the same edition of a daily newspaper.)

Strong poem

Stripped and humiliated

Frog-marched through the jungle

Fear in hearts

Retaining reserve power

Protest.

The most powerful feature is

A one-woman opposition

In control

Panic ends

Win at last

VICTORY

The boy's done good!

13 Literary Strengths and Weaknesses

Adolescents and adults can approach the topic with the following exercise. In order to find out what strength and weakness mean, they could try to seek advice from well-known personalities. What quotations can they find in literature? What sort of definitions of strength and weakness are contained in the quotes? Group members are encouraged to search for 'powerful sayings' in books and collections of quotations. For example:

Strength is only realised through hurdles that it can overcome. (Kant)

The strongest is most powerful on his own. (Schiller: *Wilhelm Tell*)

Frailty, thy name is woman. (Shakespeare: *Hamlet*)

All brutality has its origin in weakness. (Seneca)

Ignorance is strength. (Orwell)

What are the writers trying to say? What does the group think?

(14) Fancy Talk

The introduction to the topic does not always need to be serious: fun and humour can lighten the access to human strengths and weaknesses. First, the group collects sayings and lines, especially nonsense lines to do with strengths as well as weaknesses. For example:

Girl power!

Porridge makes you strong.

Going weak at the knees.

Behind every powerful man is a strong woman.

Power to the people.

This exercise could be carried out as a fancy talk competition. The group is divided into sub-groups of three to four members. Each sub-group has to come up with sayings and then agree on the most original one. All sub-groups then present their saying to the rest of the group. Secret voting is used to allocate points to each saying. Each group member has five points to give, which they can either use to give to one saying, or divide between a number of sayings. Group members are not allowed to give any points to their own saying.

(15) Powerful Body Language

Everybody writes down a 'strong' feeling (happy, self-content, and so on), or a 'strong' behaviour (to be superior to somebody, to show courage, and so on) on a piece of paper. The pieces of paper are then folded up and collected in a box. Group members take it in turns to draw a piece of paper and express the feeling or behaviour through mime, gesture and movement. The rest of the group has to guess what it might be.

What was easy to mime, what more difficult? What was easy to guess, what more difficult? What did group members feel when they were expressing 'strong' feelings or behaviours, especially when they themselves maybe tended not to be that strong themselves? Does 'powerful' body language make you feel strong?

(16) A Strong Person

For this exercise a large piece of paper with an outline of a person is required. A group member can lie on a large piece of paper on the floor and another group member can trace around them.

Together, all group members then think of different human strengths and enter them at appropriate places on the outline. For example:

◆ Head: intelligence, positive thoughts
◆ Arms: strong muscles
◆ Hands: can carry things, can caress
◆ Torso: warm heart, empathy
◆ Legs: mobility, speed
◆ Feet: standing one's ground, standing up for oneself

Afterwards, everybody studies the 'strong person'. Does this sort of person exist in real life? Would it be desirable? Which human strengths do the group think are of most importance? Why?

17 What Makes Men and Women Strong?

Generally, there are different points of view on what makes a strong woman and what makes a strong man. Group members work on their own to complete the sentences: 'Women are strong when …'; 'Men are strong when …'. At least five sentence completions should be found for each sex. The statements are then brought together, and the images of strong men and women are compared. What is considered as strength in a woman? What in a man? Are there differences in the images of men and women as seen by the female and male group members? What reasons are given? Are these reasons justified?

18 Strong Men and Women

Which women and which men do group members consider to be strong or powerful? At least three examples should be given for each sex. Examples can be personally known to the individual, or they can be public personalities or historical figures.

Which women and men were named? Why are they examples of strength and/or power? Are they role models for group members' behaviours, or could they become role models?

19 My Strong Ideal

For this exercise you need newspapers, magazines, brochures, scissors, glue, and one piece of paper per person. Group members are encouraged to choose pictures or text from the materials that particularly appeal to them, or represent how they view their own personality. Using the cuttings they then create a collage entitled 'My Strong Ideal'.

Afterwards, the collages are presented to the group and discussed. Own preferences and wishes become clear. The distanced medium of the collage requires the individuals to be less open and direct than, for example, free text or drawings. This makes this exercise particularly suitable for groups where the group members are not yet very familiar with each other.

20) Powerful Interviews

It is not only the viewpoints of the group, but also opinions on the topic of strength from outside the group that can enrich the discussion within the group.

The group is divided into pairs, and the members are asked to go outside with a pad of paper or, where available, a tape recorder, and to ask people they meet the following questions:

◆ How would you define human strength?
◆ What character traits do women and men have to show in order for you to consider them to be strong?

Anybody available can be asked, including staff working in the building (for example, teachers, porters, caretakers, office staff, cleaners, catering staff) in which the group meet, as well as other visitors to the building.

Information collected from the interviews is then evaluated in a group setting. What definitions of strength come to light? Do different professional groups have different opinions? Do the opinions of men and women differ? Did the group members discover new aspects that they had not taken into consideration up to now?

Getting to Know Your Own Strengths

The concept of self-confidence grew out of the philosophical ideas of an individual's self-awareness and self-consciousness. Included in this is the awareness of one's own abilities, strengths and weaknesses. In this context, self-awareness and self-confidence are initially value-free. To have self-awareness does not necessarily mean that one values oneself, acts with confidence and is strong. The knowledge and awareness of oneself can, however, be a first step towards this goal, because the behaviour of a person is particularly dependent on the way they sees themselves.

The perception, knowledge and recognition of oneself have an impact on the way we deal with ourselves. They also influence our judgement of others, and determine interpersonal relationships. Lack of confidence in oneself is often linked with expectations of failure and devaluation of oneself.

Many people have unrealistic expectations of themselves as well as of others. With regard to themselves, they only recognise their own weaknesses, and therefore consider themselves as weak. Other people are seen as the strong ones; that is to say, they consider what they see as signs of self-esteem and strength. Observation of self and others, as well as self-reflection, are necessary conditions for building self-confidence and self-esteem. Here it is particularly important to take a positive approach, and to get to know and accept positive abilities. Unfortunately, to see and describe oneself in a positive light is often seen as self-importance, and is often linked with feelings of guilt. However, only those who value themselves can truly fulfil their potential.

By getting to know oneself and others better and recognising individual strengths, esteem and social trust increase. If one is able to hold oneself in high esteem, one becomes less dependent on the judgment of others, and can then deal with others in a less inhibited manner.

The following games and exercises start with the often different abilities of individuals, and try to bring about an increase in self-confidence and self-esteem by getting them to know and articulate their own possibilities, abilities and wishes.

21) I am Strong Stephanie

The group is seated in a circle and members take it in turns to introduce themselves and their strengths. They say their names and also a 'strong' characteristic: for example, 'I am helpful Linda'; 'I am fast Michael'. The game becomes more difficult when members have to repeat the names of those members who have had their turn before saying their own name. For example: 'This is helpful Harriet, this is fast Michael and I am happy Tim'. It becomes even more difficult when the 'strong' characteristic has to start with the same initial letter as the person's own first name: 'This is helpful Harriet, this is fast Fred and I am strong Stephanie'.

22 I Can Do That Well

The group is seated in a circle. One group member starts, and names something they can do well. Then it is the turn of the next person on the left, who also has to name something they can do well. This continues until every member has had a turn. For example: 'I am good at baking cakes', 'I am a good organiser', 'I am a computer expert' and 'I am good at doing puzzles'.

Using these statements, the group can then play 'Moving Chairs'. An empty chair is added to the circle, and the person to the left of the chair starts: 'The chair on my right is vacant, and I wish to fill it with someone who is good at baking cakes'.

What does it feel like to say something positive about yourself? What does it feel like to be approached by someone else mentioning it?

23) I Can – I Can't

We all have strengths as well as weaknesses. In this game the group is seated in a circle. A volunteer begins and first names something they can do well, and then something they cannot do so well. The game is finished when everybody has had a turn. For example: 'I am good at getting up early. I am not so good at managing money', 'I am a good timekeeper. I am not so good at keeping things tidy'.

Which statement was easier to make, the positive or the negative one?

(24) I Like to …

The group is seated in a circle or semi-circle. Group members take it in turns to stand up and mime something that they like doing: for example, playing computer games or volleyball. Instead of miming something they like, group members could mime something they are good at, or both. Was the self-portrayal difficult? Could everybody think of something immediately?

25 I Can Do Something and I Like it

Each group member notes down five skills on a piece of paper. For example:

1 I am good at maths.
2 I am good with people.
3 I am good at dealing with failure.
4 I am always on time.
5 I am a good letter-writer.

Then everybody chooses the one skill they like best. For example: 'The best thing I like is that I am good with people'.

Was it difficult thinking of five positive skills? Was it easy or difficult to decide on one of the skills? Why was a particular skill chosen in preference to the others?

Group members are welcome to show or read out their piece of paper to the rest of the group. Are the others surprised? Would they have named the same skills? Or did they have a different image of that group member? What and why?

26 I Am – I Can – I Have

Each group member has a small piece of card stuck to their back. Written on the cards are the sentence beginnings 'I am …', 'I can …' and 'I have …'. Now everybody takes a pen and walks around the room, completing each other's sentences with 'strong' statements that suit the particular group member. The game is finished when all sentences have been completed. Everybody then takes off their card and reads what strengths have been assigned to them by the others. Writers remain anonymous, because this is likely to make it easier to tell a person something positive that they may not dare to say face-to-face.

How did group members feel during the game? How do they feel now they have read their cards? Are they surprised by what others have said about them? Do they agree with the statements?

(27) I am Proud of Myself

The group is seated in a circle and talks about the fact that every human being has value and can be proud of themselves. An appropriate piece of text, a song or a picture can be used as a lead-in to the topic. Afterwards, group members are asked to complete the sentence, 'I am proud of myself because …'

To speak openly of one's own strengths requires considerable self-confidence, but also *promotes* self-confidence. No one should be forced to say something, but everybody should be given the opportunity to do so.

What did group members feel during the exercise? Have they learned something new about others? How did they feel after they said something about themselves?

28 What I Like About Me

For most people to become aware of their own strengths is an unfamiliar or even uncomfortable feeling. It is even more difficult to do this in the presence of others. In order to practise appropriate self-praise, every group member chooses a partner whom they trust. Then they spend three minutes telling each other what they like about themselves.

Afterwards, the exercise is discussed in the group setting. How did group members feel while talking about themselves, and how did they feel when listening to the other person talking about themselves?

The difference between 'holding oneself in high esteem' and 'boasting' should be worked out.

29　My Strengths – My Weaknesses

Body outlines are a good way of creating personal access to the topic. A handout with the outline of a body and prompts for reflection on individual strengths and weaknesses is handed out:

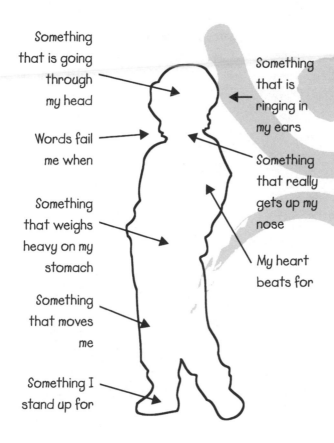

Something that is going through my head

Words fail me when

Something that weighs heavy on my stomach

Something that moves me

Something I stand up for

Something that is ringing in my ears

Something that really gets up my nose

My heart beats for

When you are working with a group of children, their own body outlines can be used. The group is divided into pairs, and each pair is given two large pieces of paper. Each child then takes it in turn to lie on a piece of paper and the other child traces around them.

When everybody has completed their piece of paper, the outlines are presented to the whole group. First of all, the group can guess which outline belongs to which person. Afterwards, the opportunity is used to discuss the strengths and weaknesses that have come out of this exercise. How do group members see themselves? How are they seen by others?

30 A Powerful Model

Everybody draws an object that they like, and that they can identify with: for example, a tree, a flower, a motorbike or an aeroplane. Then they write characteristics that they value in themselves into or next to the component parts of their object. For example, 'stability' could be written by the roots of a tree, 'loyalty' next to the leaves, 'enthusiasm for new things' next to the wheels of the motorbike, and so on.

When introducing the exercise, attention should also be drawn to characteristics that may not feature at the top of our consciousness, and may not be valued as much in today's success-focused society, such as loyalty and capacity for enthusiasm, kindness, consideration and so on.

If group members wish, they can exhibit their model. Did they discover something new about themselves and others? Did they discover undreamed-of abilities?

(31) My Name – My Programme

The letters of one's first name can be used to discover or highlight desired 'strong' characteristics or abilities in oneself. For example:

M	mellow	T	tolerant
I	intelligent	I	imaginative
K	kind	N	natural
E	energetic	A	active

It can be a bit more difficult, but at least as much fun, to try to make a phrase or sentence out of a name. For example:

M	Mike	T	Tina
I	is	I	initiates
K	king	N	numerous
E	electric.	A	activities.

These personal attributes and sentences are posted up on a flipchart and read out. They can be discussed and commented on, but this is not essential. Do the associations really have something to do with the person in question? Or was it all about finding words that fitted the letters?

(32) I-texts

In literature, it is easy to find 'I-texts' in quotations, pieces of prose or poems, for example: 'I think, therefore I am' (Descartes); 'I am the state' (Louis XIV, King of France); 'After all, the only reason why one continuously thinks of the own self is that we have to live with our own self much more consistently than with any other' (Cesare Pavese).

> *Sometimes*
> Sometimes she comes to me
> when my head
> is already so full
> I think
> my mind
> can't handle
> another thought.
> …
> I wonder if she knows
> how much
> I miss her …
> this girl
> that I used to be.
> (Flavia Weedn)

Group members are encouraged to collect and read 'I-texts'. After that they can write their own 'I-text'.

The texts are then presented to the group at a subsequent meeting. This can be done anonymously if group members are not familiar enough with each other. Texts can be discussed by the group, but this is not essential.

33 Powerful Pixies

Personal strengths can be described in a particularly poetic way by using a 'pixie'. A pixie is a poem which consists of 11 words that are distributed across five lines, as follows: one word, two words, three words, four words, one word. For example:

William
a boy
is very strong
and proud and self-confident
really!

Selina
a girl
clever and compassionate
knows what she wants
honest!

Ask group members to create their own. Using this format, they can communicate something about themselves. Did they do that? Was it easy or difficult to portray themselves so positively?

34 I am Looking at Myself

One is only strong if one can accept one's looks and face for what they are. For this exercise, everybody requires a mirror in addition to paper and pencil. As an introduction to the topic, questions such as the following are asked:

- 'What makes a face expressive and interesting?'
- 'What is the difference between a beautiful and an interesting face?'
- 'Do you sometimes feel like hiding your face? Why?'
- 'How well do you really know your face?'

Our face is unique. It tells a lot about the family we come from and that we are proud of. Maybe the eyes are our mother's, the chin our father's, the high forehead comes from our grandmother, our great grandfather also had that shape of earlobe …

Everybody now studies their face in the mirror. What shape is my face? Round or square, oval or pointed? What does my forehead look like? What about my hairline? What shape are my eyes? What colour are they? Have I got thick or thin eyebrows? And so on.

The main features of the faces are written down, and then discussed. Have I learned something new about my face? What makes it expressive, especially if it is not a face that would be considered beautiful in the traditional sense? Maybe I have an energetic chin? A particularly intense look? A funny liver spot on the cheek? What do I like about my face, and would not like to have any different?

35 Feeling All Right in Your Own Body

One can only develop personal strength and self-confidence if one can befriend one's own body. But who actually really knows their own body? A fantasy journey into the body can be of assistance. The journey can start when all group members are sitting in a relaxed position on their chairs. The group leader speaks:

'Close your eyes and try to imagine you are looking at yourself in the mirror. Look at yourself closely. Let your eyes move slowly from head to toes – and slowly back up again. Look more closely at your head. What does it look like? What shape is it? What does your hair look like? Have you got your favourite hairstyle today? Or what is your favourite hairstyle? Look at your face: forehead, eyes, nose, cheeks, mouth, chin … look at your neck and your body … How big is it? How strong is it? How long are your arms? How big are your hands? How soft are they? Look at your fingers. Are they narrow and long, or more short and friendly? Look at your legs. How long are they? Have you got big feet or little feet? What are you wearing? What are your favourite clothes? Imagine you are wearing your favourite outfit. What colours do you like particularly? What do you need to wear to really feel good? What makes you feel strange and uncomfortable? Have another good look at yourself. You are just right as you are. You are unique. There is only one person on Earth who is like you. You are important. Remember that when you are feeling down and you don't believe in yourself. Recall the image of what you are like now. You are unique. You *are* strong. Now slowly open your eyes and rejoin the group.'

Afterwards, time needs to be given so that everybody who wants to can talk about their experiences during the fantasy journey. Contributions must be on a voluntary basis only.

(36) A Family to be Proud of

The family can provide a lot of strength. There is something in every family, a special event or person, that one can be proud of. However, we are not always aware of this, so we need to look for something special.

Every group member brings in a family object (or a picture of an object) that represents something meaningful that the member can be proud of, and tells the group the story behind the object. Examples:

◆ A photograph of (great) grandmother during or after the war
◆ An old family Bible, which has been in the family and passed from generation to generation for the last 100 years
◆ A photocopy of the certificate that mother received for her voluntary services to the local sports club
◆ A cake baked by father especially for the occasion after he got home from work last night.

Who learned something new about their family in preparing for this exercise? Did everybody know how much reason they had to be proud of their family? How are they feeling now?

37 Journey to Your Own Strengths

A good way to approach personal strengths is through a fantasy journey. Once everybody has assumed a relaxed position, the journey can start. Words and content can be changed, depending on age and needs of the group. The group leader speaks:

'Close your eyes. Take your thoughts back a few weeks … months … years … in your life. Go back to situations when you felt happy, self-confident, able. What did you see … what images? … what colours? What did you hear? Which voices were particularly pleasant? What was your voice like? What smells do you remember? What did you feel? What did you do that made you feel so good? What was it that gave you such a feeling of well-being and strength? Try to find a word or a sentence that describes that strength… . Did you find something appropriate? Now take three deep breaths … stretch your whole body … and rejoin our group. Open your eyes.

'Now write down the word or the sentence that you found for your strength. Or you can draw a picture. Choose colours that go with your strength. Such symbols of strength can be, for example, a lion or a rising sun.'

Afterwards, group members can talk about the experiences they had on their journey. They should try to remember the word, the sentence or the image and colours that they found for their strength, and recall them when they are in need of strength.

38 Good Feelings

We react differently to things, events and people as far as our emotions are concerned. For this game the group is divided into small sub-groups, which are asked to write down or draw what gives them good feelings, or what makes them feel strong and self-confident. On a second piece of paper, they note down what causes feelings of weakness and inferiority.

Afterwards, the whole group discusses what causes good feelings and what causes bad feelings. Why is this so? Can we change this?

The group can also be asked to take stock each night for a few days. (What made me feel good today? When did I feel strong?) Each night, at least three things should be recorded. This is not really difficult: with a bit of thought, everybody can come up with three things. For example:

1 Praise from a teacher
2 My little brother giving me a kiss
3 Home-made pancake.

Those who take stock every night will eventually be surprised by their own strengths.

(39) Friendly Interview

The group is seated in a circle. Two group members move with their chairs into the middle of the circle, and interview each other. They take it in turns to ask each other questions about their personal strengths. Everybody is allowed five questions and five answers, then a new pair moves into the middle for a friendly interview. And so on until everyone has had a turn. Possible questions:

1 What do you like doing best?
2 What can you do best?
3 What do you like about yourself?
4 What do you own that you are really proud of?
5 What is your best subject at school?

It can be a good idea to brainstorm lots of positive questions prior to the exercise, to make sure that questions really are only about strengths, and to ensure that the same questions are not repeated in each interview.

There should be an opportunity after the exercise to talk about feelings during the interviews. What did it feel like to ask the questions? What did it feel like to be interviewed? What did it feel like to observe and listen?

40 Hot Seat

This is a well-known exercise. The group is seated in a circle. A group member takes a chair into the middle of the circle, sits down and moves with the chair from one group member to the next. Every time they stop in front of a group member, that member has to tell the person in the hot seat something they like about them. The person in the hot seat is not allowed to say anything themselves, but has to accept the compliments in silence.

How difficult is it to accept only praise? What is it like to tell someone something positive, even though one normally does not actually like or know that person very well?

41 Powerful Circle Conversations

The group members form an outer and an inner circle, so that pairs are always facing each other. Listening for a call by the leader, little by little, they tell each other about their respective abilities. After every call, the inner circle moves on one. The first call could be: 'Talk about something that you can do well.' After about two minutes, the inner circle moves on one person to the right. Now comes the second call: 'Talk about something that others like about you.' The inner circle moves on. Two new group members are facing each other. Other topics could include the following:

◆ A strength of one of my family members
◆ Something I particularly enjoy doing
◆ An event that left me feeling very satisfied
◆ Something nice I did for someone
◆ Something special I did at school
◆ Something I did well today
◆ The most difficult situation I have had to master up to now
◆ A situation where I showed courage.

There are many topics, so the game does not need to finish until everybody has arrived back with their original partner. Afterwards the group talks about the game. Was it difficult to tell so many positive things about yourself? How did you feel doing that? What did you learn about the others? Did you have any idea that there were so many brilliant people in the group?

(42) I Like Being a Girl – I Like Being a Boy

The group divides into a girl sub-group and a boy sub-group. The girl group has to come up with as many reasons as possible to complete the sentence: 'I like being a girl because …'. The boy group does exactly the same thing: 'I like being a boy because …'. Each group notes down their reasons on a piece of flipchart paper.

Completed flipcharts are then evaluated by the whole group. What sort of arguments did the respective groups come up with? How wide is the breadth of arguments? Are there differences between the girls and the boys? What are they?

43 Girls and Boys Play Powerful Roles

For this exercise the group splits into boy and girl sub-groups. The following questions are then discussed within each sub-group:

◆ Can you think of a situation when you felt particularly strong?
◆ Does being strong mean to be superior to others?
◆ Is it possible to be strong on your own?

Both sub-groups note down their main points on a piece of flipchart paper.

Afterwards, the results from the two discussions are picked out as a central theme by the whole group. This works best when girls and boys role-play situations for each other where they have felt particularly strong. What comments does the other sex have in each case? Are there differences between the sexes? What are they?

44 Blowing Your Own Trumpet

Every group member writes an advertisement for themselves. The advertisement is supposed to promote the person, highlighting special talents, positive characteristics and behaviours.

When all advertisements are complete, a 'market' is created where everybody has to stand up to discuss the content of their advert. They may have to provide more specific information and promote themselves in response to specific enquiries. Embellishing and supplementing information provided in the adverts is allowed, as long as members stick to the truth.

What experiences did group members have when formulating their 'self-advertisement'? How did they get on at the 'market'?

45 **Wish and Reality**

A list is provided with 10 to 15 positive and desired attributes (these will varty according to the age group). For example, for teenagers these could be:

clever	brave	helpful	sporty
persistent	creative	attractive	cool
decisive	popular	strong	pretty
funny	affectionate	friendly	

The group has to answer the question, 'What would you particularly like to be like?' by picking five of the characteristics from the list. Those five characteristics represent their ideal.

Now the list is supplemented with some negative attributes that are not desirable in that same age group, for example:

fearful	weak	stubborn	aggressive
restless	slow	unpopular	ugly

From this extended list of positive and negative attributes, group members are asked to select the five that best answer the question: 'What do you think you are really like?' Ideal and self-image are then compared and contrasted. How do they differ?

The exercise can also be carried out separately for the female and male members of the group. How do the ideals and self-images of the different sexes differ?

46 That's Me

Every group member creates an 'I-page' or 'I-poster'. They stick their photograph on to a large piece of paper or cardboard. Underneath or next to it they write their personal description. Group members are encouraged to include anything in their personal description that they think of as important or a strength with regard to their own person and want to tell others about, for example: age, name, hobbies, favourite food, favourite animal, and so on.

Of course, members can also decide as a group what information should definitely be included in their personal description. They can even design a particular form that everybody then has to complete. For example:

Name _____

Age _____ Height _____

Hair colour _____

Eye colour _____

My favourite pastime _____

_____

What I can do best _____

My best qualities are _____

My most important aim is _____

The group members are then encouraged to compare their 'I-pages'. Who have they got similarities with? Who is totally different? Did they know that before?

The completed 'I-pages' can be nicely arranged and compiled into a group book, 'That's Us', and thus serve as a catalyst for more group work. Where a group is together for a long time, the exercise can be repeated every so often. How have individual group members changed? Have they got closer to their aims? Or have their aims changed?

47 My Personal Coat of Arms

Special talents and skills can be symbolised by objects, animals, signs and so on. Initially, the group collects ideas for such drawings. For example, a lion may symbolise special strength; two hands touching may stand for helpfulness, a sword for courage, a horse for speed. Maybe there is even someone whose family has a coat of arms, and who can explain its significance.

All group members are given a piece of paper with the outline of a coat of arms.

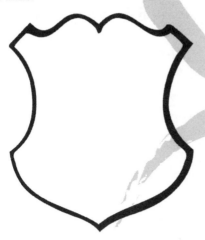

Group members are then given the task of creating their own coat of arms by drawing in pictures and symbols that tell something about their particular strengths and abilities. The completed coats of arms are then presented and discussed by the whole group. What do the coats of arms tell us about the skills of the individual group members?

48 Gathered Strengths

Self-esteem always needs some looking after and support. A good way of strengthening self-esteem is to collect all the 'strong' worksheets and all the 'powerful' drawings that every group member has been completing during groupwork time. Looking at their work will stimulate group members to recall positive insights about themselves, and thus stabilise the progress already made. A special folder could be created to store worksheets and drawings. The cover sheet of the folder could be decorated with a self-portrait and/or an individual symbol of strength. Every group member should come up with a truly personal symbol that they alone have.

Gaining Strength – Showing Strength

Positive self-esteem reduces insecurity, decreases fear and, with that, the tendency to behave in a socially unacceptable manner. Freedom of decision-making and self-control in situations that used to trigger dependent, uncertain or even aggressive behaviour based on fear are made possible through the development of self-assured behaviour patterns. Self-confident people are able to perceive and respect their own as well as others' limitations. They can communicate clearly their needs and desires to others. They have learned to voice and accept negative things, too, without being led to develop feelings of helplessness, fear and guilt.

Self-confidence and strength grow from experiencing successful activities. A person derives positive feelings from everything they succeed in. Therefore acting in a self-confident manner is perceived by the person in many ways as encouraging and motivating. Additional recognition and confirmation increase the effect.

The following games and exercises are aimed particularly at the ability to assert oneself in a self-confident manner; in other words:

◆ Recognising one's own needs
◆ Having the courage to voice these
◆ Asserting oneself appropriately.

The following methods are used to achieve this:

◆ Self-observation
◆ Self-expression
◆ Positive self-programming
◆ Self-reinforcement
◆ Self-control.

49 Shaking off Weaknesses

We have to cast off our weaknesses so we can gain in strength. Sometimes a simple 'shaking off' can help. Everybody stands up and finds a space where they can move freely. They shake out their arms and hands, legs and feet, their whole body. Everything unpleasant, all feelings of inferiority, all bad thoughts, all fears are shaken off. Everybody imagines that they are loosening up and becoming more carefree – free and open for new strength.

50 Pushing away Weaknesses

We can push away our weaknesses. Group members are asked to imagine that they are packing all their bad feelings and thoughts, their worries and fears in a big bag. They then scrunch up this bag and press it together tightly in their right hand. They close the hand into a fist, tighter and tighter, until all the bad feelings and worries have become tiny. Then they open their fist and simply throw away those concentrated bad thoughts and feelings. Afterwards, they shake out the hand. If there are still weaknesses and worries left, the whole procedure is repeated with the left hand.

51 Dream Yourself Strong

If someone is not strong already, they can at least dream themselves strong for the time being. A fantasy journey can lead into such strong dreams. Group members are asked to find a relaxed sitting position. The instruction for the fantasy journey can then be read out by the group leader. It can go something like this:

'Imagine a wonderful place, a place where you would most like to be … a place where you feel happy. What sort of things are there? What can you see? What can you hear? What can you smell? What can you feel? Make yourself comfortable … stretch … enjoy the space … Dream yourself strong and beautiful. What do you look like? What do you especially like about your appearance? What do the others like? Which of your characteristics do you especially like? Think about it … You are strong and cool. What else are you? Make a mental list. What do others value in you? What can you do particularly well? What else can you do? What do others admire in you? If you think about everything you have just seen in front of you, there is a lot that is special and lovable about you. Tell yourself: I am lovable. I like myself. Say it again: I am lovable. I like myself. And again: I am lovable. I like myself. Think about this exercise next time you are feeling low or you don't believe in yourself. Tell yourself in your thoughts: I am lovable. I like myself. Say it until you feel better. And now, rejoin the group.'

Afterwards, allow time to talk about what group members experienced during the fantasy journey. Alternatively, they can write down or draw characteristics they dreamt up for themselves. They can then put up that text or picture in a place of their choice – for example, by the mirror at home or above their bed – and gain strength and self-confidence from looking at it when they need to.

(52) Self-Confirmation

We can treat ourselves badly and discourage ourselves, but we can also be good to ourselves and make ourselves more determined. First of all, the group discusses what it is we do when we treat ourselves badly and what we can do to make ourselves more determined. For example, we treat ourselves badly:

◆ When we continually worry about what could happen
◆ When, with every new task, we say immediately: 'Oh, I can't do that'
◆ When we don't allow ourselves to be happy.

We make ourselves more determined, for example:

◆ When we say: 'Oh, I can handle that'
◆ When we treat ourselves to something nice to eat
◆ When we do something we have always wanted to do.

What makes us more determined differs from person to person. We can find out what it is by, for example, going on a guided fantasy journey. Once group members have made themselves comfortable and are breathing quietly, the instruction could be read out. For example, the group leader may say:

'Close your eyes. Let your breath move quietly and evenly. Little by little, a warm light is growing out of the dark.

Gradually, you can make out more and more. In the light, you see a good fairy. She gives you a friendly smile. She calls you by your name. She tells you: "I know you very well. Sometimes, you don't treat yourself that well. You are unfriendly to yourself. You cause yourself to feel bad. I want to help you to recognise three things that are good for you and that let you feel self-confident and strong. You only need to listen deep into yourself. You know what is good for you. You are listening deep into yourself". All of a sudden, you know what the good fairy means. The three things that are good for you and make you more determined are, one … , two … , three … You repeat to yourself the three things. You want to say thank you to the good fairy, but she is not there any more. The light in the dark has disappeared. You are alone again. Open your eyes slowly. Come back to the group.'

What were the three things that were good for group members, and made them more determined? After repeating them to themselves, they can write them down. If they like, they can tell the group about them.

53   Superman and Superwoman

The identification with a 'strong' fantasy figure can provide self-confidence and strength. The group members think about 'strong' role models they know whom they would like to emulate. The names are noted down on a flipchart or whiteboard. Such 'strong' figures could be Superman, Rambo, Robin Hood, and so on. Everybody chooses a hero or heroine, and visits them with the help of a fantasy journey. The instruction for the journey might be as follows:

'Sit on your chair and relax. Close your eyes. You are walking along a street. At the end of the street there is a memorial. It is a fantastic memorial. On top of it stands your hero or heroine. Who is standing on your memorial? Can you recognise them clearly? Your hero or your heroine lifts you up on to the memorial. They put their hand on your shoulder. You can feel how you are getting stronger through their touch. You are gaining in strength and self-confidence, just like your hero or heroine. They are saying to you: "I want to give you some of my strength. You will be like me, courageous, self-confident, strong. When you are feeling low, think of me. I will help you." You stay at the memorial for a little while longer. You are feeling strong and self-assured, just like your hero or heroine.'

Back in the group, group members draw a picture of themselves in the guise of their hero or heroine. Afterwards, the completed pictures are put up in the room. Whoever likes to can tell the group why they have chosen a particular figure to identify with. What is so remarkable about them?

54 My Magic Finger

When required use the following exercise to strengthen self-confidence. Imagine the ring finger of your left hand is your magic finger. Every time you find yourself in a situation where you are feeling uncertain and weak, you rub your magic finger with the fingers of your right hand. Everything that you tell yourself while you are rubbing your magic finger will make come true. For example, tell yourself: 'Everybody in this room is nice to me' – and everybody will be nice to you; 'I will talk with a confident voice now' – and you start talking with a confident voice.

If your wish does not come true immediately, tell it to yourself a second time. You may also need to say it again a third and fourth time before it works. You will see, your wish will come true.

55   Weak Sides

Many things that we do not feel strong enough for are, in the end, not so bad after all. Many fears sort themselves out. Often it is enough simply to take a little more time. The following 'magic' can also help. All problems that come up during the course of a week are written down individually on loose pieces of paper, which are filed in a folder or put into an envelope. At the end of the week, the 'weak' pages are checked. What has sorted itself out and can be thrown away? For which problems have group members since come up with a solution? What is left; where do they need help?

Unresolved problems that are left are discussed by the group. Together, the group tries to come up with solutions. The conversation within the group can provide the support and strength that is needed by the particular group members to gain the courage to tackle and resolve their problems.

56) If I Had a Magic Wand 1

A magic wand is always good for conjuring up strength when needed. It can also be introduced with the help of a fantasy journey:

'Make yourself comfortable and close your eyes. Imagine you have a magic wand. You can use it to conjure up any abilities that you would like to have. Think for a while, which abilities would you like? Do you know now what you would like to be like? Think for a moment about which of those is the most important one for you. Wave your magic wand and say it to yourself in your thoughts. If you don't know how to deal with a particular situation, simply ask your magic wand. It will help you. Now come back to the group and open your eyes.'

If they wish, group members can now talk about those things that went through their heads during the exercise. They can also write them down or draw them. They can keep them somewhere safe and look at them again when they need a magic wand.

If I Had a Magic Wand 2

The group is seated in a circle. All members talk about things that they have difficulties with, and about abilities that they would like to have. The conversation can, for example, take up a subject of topical interest: there has been friction within the group, a group member has been expelled, and so on. To conclude the conversation, three group members are chosen, and awarded a 'magic wand'. This can be a role of paper, a ruler or something similar that looks like a stick. Holding the magic wand, they move around the circle and touch individual group members who were particularly involved in the preceding conflict, and put a spell on them. For example, they may say:

◆ 'I put a spell on you. You don't have to get involved in fights with others. When there is an argument you will stay calm and cool.'

◆ 'I put a spell on you. You are a good friend.'

'Strengthening' problem-solving that can easily be accepted is offered with the help of the magic wand.

58 Compliments and Criticisms

Being able to accept and give compliments and criticism requires a good deal of self-confidence. Many people feel uncomfortable with it. The following exercise can make them 'stronger'.

The group members are given small pieces of paper on which they write their names. The pieces of paper are shuffled and put in a bag or large envelope. Then everybody chooses one. If someone draws their own name they quickly put it back and draw another one. The group now sits in a circle. One after the other, they have to stand up and make a compliment, as well as communicate a critical remark to the group member whose name they have drawn. The group member who is being addressed tries to accept both compliment and criticism with honest agreement. The compliment could, for example, be responded to with comments such as:

◆ I'm so pleased.
◆ I like to hear that.
◆ That feels good.

Criticisms can be responded to, depending on whether the member considers them to be justified or unjustified, with comments such as:

◆ Yes, you are absolutely right. I am sorry.
◆ I really did not want to hurt anybody.
◆ It is good of you to tell me that.

If someone is unable to say anything, they can simply give a friendly smile or a serious nod.

How difficult was it to hear compliments and criticisms, and to respond to them without protest or opposition? How difficult was it to voice directly compliments and criticisms? What did group members feel during the exercise? What are they feeling now they have had their 'go'? Which answers and reactions were particularly appropriate? These comments could be written down and then, so that everybody can remember them, be repeated again.

59 Strong Stories

The group brainstorms a list of 'strong' characteristics or activities. From this list, every group member chooses five characteristics that they would love to have themselves: for example, self-confident, tall, courageous, winning, praise. They then write 'I-stories' that contain all these words. For example:

> Our class had agreed to a football game with another class. I really wanted to play, but what could I do to be put forward for the team? When the team was being selected, I made myself really tall and self-confidently said to our PE teacher: 'I am a good football player.' Consequently, I was allowed to play reserve. When I was brought on I courageously confronted my opposite number – and actually prevented a goal. Our class won the game. And I got a lot of praise.

The stories are then read out. Which ones were the 'strongest'? A rule could also be introduced that everybody uses the same five words. Which of the stories is now the strongest?

60 Running the Gauntlet

The group members face each other in two rows. They then take turns to walk down between the two rows. They are encouraged to walk slowly and keep themselves upright, look at the others, keep a friendly smile and say 'Hello', and not be provoked by unpleasant words and gestures. The group members in the two rows have to try to unsettle the member running the gauntlet by laughing, taunting, pulling faces and gesturing.

How difficult was it to keep calm, to remain friendly, and not to speed up while walking?

(61) Acting with Self-confidence

There is an interaction between body posture and self-confidence. Someone who is self-confident generally communicates that through their body posture. However, this can also work the other way around, where self-confident body posture can help to increase a person's strength and self-confidence.

Individual group members introduce themselves (voluntarily) to the group. How did their body posture come across? Self-assured or more uncertain? Natural or more affected? Bored or more open? Which features of someone's body posture can tell something about the inner attitude of the person? Through experimental role-play and conversation, the features of a self-confident body posture are worked out:

◆ Upright with head lifted
◆ Eyes keeping eye contact
◆ Arms hanging loose down the body
◆ Both feet firmly on the floor
◆ Friendly facial expression.

To finish off, self-confident body posture is practised in pairs. One group member models a self-confident body posture, the other member mirrors it. Roles are changed from time to time. The exercise is finished when both partners can act with self-confidence. If an instant or digital camera is available, photos are taken of group members with that posture. Looking at the photo can reassure when necessary: 'I can come across as self-confident.'

(62) Standing Tall Like a Tree

A self-assured posture can also be strengthened through a guided fantasy: Group members are asked to stand up. The instruction can then be read out as follows:

'Imagine you are a tree. The soles of your feet have roots that grow into the earth and are anchored firmly into the ground. Experiment to find out how you can best stand firmly so that you don't lose your balance even in a storm. Lean forwards, to the side, backwards, as far as possible, but without lifting your heels. Your heels stay firmly on the ground. Imagine your heels are the joint from which the tree sways. Try to find at which point the tree is most stable. Find a perfectly balanced position, where you can stand, but also move freely, without feeling any tension in your neck, in your shoulders, in your back, in your feet. Enjoy your personal position of perfect balance and perfect stability. Memorise this position. Keep it in your memory. You can always create that position again. When you stand that well balanced and assured, you will yourself be balanced and self-assured.'

Afterwards, an opportunity should be given to talk about experiences during this body exercise.

(63) Advertising Campaign

This exercise can be used to demonstrate self-confidence standing up for a particular request.

The group invents fantasy products and, on index cards, notes down product names and a brief description of each product. Index cards are then shuffled and spread out face-down on the table. Each group member takes a card. One at a time, members promote the product they have chosen to the group. The rest of the group evaluates their performance in terms of originality and persuasiveness.

What does it feel like to stand in front of the group and promote a particular product? What thoughts are going through your head? How does your body respond?

64 Powerful Presentations

Acting confidently in front of a group can also be practised by giving a presentation. Every group member is given an index card, on which they note a funny or nonsense topic for a short presentation. For example:

◆ The love life of earth worms
◆ Going to school on the moon
◆ My life as a giraffe.

Cards are collected and shuffled. Each group member takes a card. If anybody gets their own card, they put it back and take a new one. The group is given five to 10 minutes to prepare their presentation. Members then take it in turns to give their presentation. Each presentation is allowed a maximum of three minutes. The rest of the group have to listen attentively and mark the presentation in terms of originality and confidence.

After all presentations have been given, the exercise is discussed by the group. How did group members feel as presenters? Do their own perceptions match the evaluation of the audience? What criteria did they use to evaluate the presentations? Was it difficult to evaluate others knowing that they would still have to present themselves?

(65) I-messages

If someone wants to make something clear, or to communicate something about themselves, that person should be sending I-messages rather than you-messages. You-messages are statements that begin with 'you', and that generally express what a person wants to say in a roundabout sort of way. Often they are hurtful or immediately trigger opposition. With I-messages, however, one tries to communicate one's own requests or feelings without attacking or hurting the other person. For example, 'You idiot!' may be meant to mean 'I am really angry with you', 'You never listen to me!' is likely to mean 'I don't feel you are taking me seriousl.', and so on.

Colloquially, we tend to use considerably more you-messages than I-messages. That is why it is important to practise formulating I-messages. The group is divided into sub-groups of three. Two members from each sub-group have a brief conversation about any topic that is not too demanding (for example: 'Where are you going on holiday this year?'). They are allowed to use only I-messages. The third person listens and, when the conversation has finished, provides feedback on whether or not they have succeeded. Then roles are swapped around.

Afterwards, experiences of the different sub-groups are discussed by the whole group.

66 Saying No

The group stands in a circle. One after the other, members step forward and say, depending on individual temperaments, a clear 'No!', possibly supported by an appropriate body movement. In order to make saying 'no' easier, questions can also be asked that can really be negated with conviction; for example: 'Do you want any more homework?' or 'Do you want cinema tickets to become more expensive?'

When everybody has practised their 'No', the group talks about which of the 'Nos' was especially successful. During discussion it should become clear that volume is not the only important feature. A quiet 'No' can be just as effective as a loud one. The important thing is that the 'No' is said clearly, with unambiguous facial expression and body posture.

In a second round, everybody tries once more to say 'No' in a way that convinces and does not allow any opposition. Of course, a third and fourth round can also be added, until the right 'No' has been found.

(67) Yes and No

Saying 'No' can be practised by all group members at the same time. This exercise is particularly suitable for children's groups.

First of all, the group is divided into pairs. Each pair agrees on who out of the two is going to say 'Yes', and who is going to say 'No'. The leader then gives a starting signal, at which one half of the group has to continuously say 'No', while the other half has to say 'Yes', until the command 'Stop' is given by the leader. In a second round, roles are reversed. In this exercise, the quiet 'No' is not appropriate: 'No' and, of course, 'Yes' have to be said loudly so they can be heard. If no one else is going to be disturbed by the noise, the group can be encouraged to shout as loudly as possible. For some people, this exercise may be the first opportunity to show the courage to counter a 'Yes' with a 'No' by shouting as loudly as possible. To say 'No' directly is often considered to be impertinent.

What was easier, saying 'Yes', or saying 'No'?

68   Giving a Piece of Your Mind

Someone who wants to hold their own ground needs to be able to communicate clearly and unambiguously refusals as well as accepting friendly words.

The group is seated in a circle. One at a time, members turn to the person on their left and communicate a brief and concise, but clear refusal, for example:

- ◆ 'I don't want to.'
- ◆ 'Get lost.'
- ◆ 'Leave me alone.'
- ◆ 'I've had enough.'

The refusals can be supported by respective gestures, such as showing a fist or threatening with a finger.

How difficult was it to behave in an unambiguously negative manner? Which expressions could also be used in real situations? Which ones would be better not?

69 I Want to

Just as with refusals and rejections, demands and requests also need to be communicated clearly and, where necessary, need to be supported argumentatively.

Again, the group is seated in a circle. One at a time, members tell the person on their left something that they really want or wish for. For example, this could be expressed as follows:

◆ 'I definitely want it.'
◆ 'I must have it.'
◆ 'I won't give in until I get it.'
◆ 'There is nothing I wish for more than …'

If possible, phrases should not be repeated.

How difficult was it to find and express insistent words for demands and requests? How do group members normally communicate their demands and requests? Are they always taken seriously? What sort of behaviours do they need to acquire in order to be able to assert themselves?

70 Good Excuses

Making up excuses can also be good training for self-assertion. It can be used to practise not being intimidated by unexpected situations, but instead to react with creative solutions.

Making up excuses is practised in pairs in front of the rest of the group. One member accuses the other of something, or points out a mistake they have made, or something similar. The other member has to try to make up a good excuse and deliver it with self-confidence. For example: 'We had a date for 11 o'clock. That was more than an hour ago.' Excuses:

◆ 'There must have been a misunderstanding. I'd written down 12 o'clock. And now it is only just a quarter to 12.'
◆ 'Oh, is it really that late already? I dropped my watch earlier on, and I have a feeling it's slow now.'
◆ 'My bus was late and that made me miss our 11 o'clock date.'

Other prompts for making excuses are, for example:

◆ 'You owe me £10. I really need the money back urgently.'
◆ 'Why didn't you tell me that you failed your maths test?'
◆ 'My best friend has told me that you are spreading a rumour that I'm talking about her behind her back. Why are you doing that?'

Is it possible to react creatively without making excuses?

(71) Self-Assertion Matters

The group divides into sub-groups of three, each of which role-play different situations where self-assertion and self-assurance matter. Two members take part in the role-play while the third observes and gives feedback on how well they succeeded in coming across as self-confident. All members take a turn in each role. If the group is not too big, role-play can also take place in front of the whole group. Scenarios could include the following:

◆ Someone has squeezed in front of you at the supermarket check-out.
◆ In the cinema, an older teenager demands that a child gets up because he is apparently sitting in the teenager's seat.
◆ A friend wants to borrow something that the other does not want him to have.

It is even better when situations from group members' everyday life can be used as scenarios. Afterwards, the group jointly works out what possibilities there are to assert oneself. For example:

◆ Rejecting demands, saying 'No'
◆ Providing reasons for one's point of view
◆ Articulating understanding.

Was it always possible to support one's own point of view? When was it easy? When was it particularly difficult?

72 Don't Put Up with Everything

Someone who is put down and treated badly by others has often not made it clear how they would like to be treated. The group members initially discuss what manners are common among their circle of friends, what is acceptable, and what they would not put up with. Afterwards, each member writes down for themselves at least three demands about how they wish to be treated by others, for example:

- I want to be treated with respect.
- I want people to listen to me.
- I don't want to be shouted at by anybody.

Individual demands are then discussed by the group. What is particularly important? What is totally unacceptable?

(73) Code of Honour

Boys and girls clarify how they wish to be treated by the other sex. For this the group initially divides into girls and boys. Each sub-group has its own discussion and has to complete the sentence: 'We want girls/boys ...' The girls could demand, for example:

◆ 'We want boys not to make fun of us.'
◆ 'We want boys to stop touching us.'

The boys could demand, for example:

◆ 'We want the girls to stop calling us names.'
◆ 'We want the girls to stop telling on us.'

Once both groups have finished their discussions, demands and wishes are read out to the whole group and discussed. Are the demands of one sub-group acceptable to the other? Are they realised in that group? How can they be realised? Are the demands made by the girls different from those made by the boys? Where do they differ?

Using the two groups' expectations of each other, a 'code of honour' can be worked out: that's how we will treat each other in the future!

74 Standing Up to Group Pressure

Standing up to group pressure requires a great deal of self-confidence and, therefore, is not always successful. Often it is even difficult to admit that one is susceptible to group pressure.

Reflection on the problem 'group pressure' can, for example, begin with an exercise that requires all group members to work individually on the following task. Think of a situation where you were subject to group pressure and tried not to give in to it. Describe the situation:

◆ What put you under pressure in that situation?
◆ How did you try not to give in to the pressure?
◆ Were you happy with yourself?

Different, individual experiences are then discussed within the group. What actually causes group pressure? What behaviours have individuals found useful in standing up to group pressure? Which behaviours work best? Which behaviours can be recommended to others?

75 Being Different

This exercise looks at ways of standing up to group pressure.

The group is seated in a circle. The same number of pieces of paper as group members are required. Most of the pieces of paper are labelled with 'Yes', and only one or two are labelled with 'No'. All pieces of paper are folded up so that it is impossible to see whether they are 'Yes' or 'No' pieces. Group members are then told: 'We now want to take an important vote. Imagine we are voting on something that is really important for the whole group. It is critical that everybody votes "Yes". You have to try to change even the last person's mind who votes "No". You now get your ballot paper, which tells you how to vote. If your paper says "Yes", you must definitely vote "Yes"; if it says "No", you must vote "No". Open your papers. Let's vote. Who is voting "Yes"? Look around and see who is voting "No". Who is voting against such an important group motion? Those voting with "No" please stand up.' The instructions can be continued as you like, in order to increase the pressure on the person(s) voting 'No'.

Afterwards, the experiences felt during the exercise are discussed. What was it like to get a 'No' piece of paper? Was it difficult to stick with 'No'? Would they have stuck with 'No' if this had been a real situation?

The vote can also be carried out using a concrete topic. For example: 'Imagine we have been offered some money for a group field trip. We have to come to a unanimous decision in order to get the money.'

(76) Done!

Situations where one has completed and achieved something are important for our self-confidence. That is why we have to make ourselves aware of such situations from time to time.

The instruction to the group could read as follows: 'I am sure that all of you have at some time achieved something that was not easy and that required you to gather all your strength. Maybe others did not realise that you had achieved something special. But you knew. Take a piece of paper and draw or paint the situation and how you handled it. It can be a representational picture. You do not have to be able to paint, though. You can express what you have achieved simply through colours and shapes.'

Afterwards, the pictures are exhibited in the room. How do they appear to others? What emotions are expressed? Anybody who would like to do so can explain their picture. What situation is it about? What was difficult about it? How was the situation handled?

77 Setting Goals

When somebody is not clear about what they are supposed to be heading for, they will also be unable to tell whether they are on the right track or not. Someone who wants to change has to set themselves concrete goals and, where possible, also set a time-frame within which they are going to achieve their goals.

Everybody notes down on a piece of paper what they would like to have changed or learned by a date three months from now, by the summer holidays or by Christmas. Goals should be clearly defined and positive. They have to be about something that can sensibly be achieved. Goals should not be too vague. So, rather than, 'I would like to become less shy', a more concrete and realistic goal could be, 'By the end of this year, I would like to learn to contribute actively to the discussions in the classroom.'

The desired behaviour can then be practised by using role-play, with group members giving each other suggestions as to how individual goals can best be realised.

Was it difficult to transform wishes into concrete behaviour goals? Are the goals truly realistic? Is it really going to be possible to meet them within the given time-frame? Or do group members tend to set goals that are too big and too complex to be realised? Or do they only ever set themselves really small goals so that they will not be disappointed? What have they learned about others during this exercise?

(78) Journey into the Future

Someone who wants to change only needs to know what they want to be like. What does the ideal of a self-assured, self-confident person look like? Using the following exercise, one can explore one's own ideal: 'Imagine you are making a journey into the future. You have aged by 10 years. How do you see yourself now? Write a brief report, beginning: "I am … years old. I …".'

Reports are posted (anonymously) in the room and read. Visions of the future are discussed. What needs to happen so that they can become reality? What actions can be taken by us to contribute to this? What sort of help is needed? Anybody who wants to do so can comment on and explain their vision of the future.

(79) Discovering Something Positive

Those who believe they are always unlucky will always be unlucky. Most things that we are experiencing as negative also have their positive sides – if we want to see them. A half-filled glass can be considered as half-empty, but also as half-full. Here is another example:

Today is Friday. The weather outlook is bad – such a shame, I won't be able to do anything on Sunday. I can forget all my plans. It will be a boring Sunday, all alone and in the bath.

Today is Friday. The weather outlook is bad, but it is another couple of days until Sunday. Maybe it will brighten up. So I'll make some plans anyway. And if it does rain, excellent. I'm due for a bit of self-pampering anyway.

Thinking positively can be practised. To do this, group members are given the following instruction: 'Practise seeing the positive. Make a list of things that haven't gone too well today, when you were "weak". Now try and see something positive in it.' An example follows:

Event: I was not selected for the football game on Sunday. Peter called me a 'weakling' in the presence of Mary.

Positive: Brilliant. I'll now have time to go swimming on Sunday. Mary never said that she liked muscle men like Peter.

Often it is difficult initially to interpret an event positively. Where did you not succeed? Here the group can help, and provide suggestions for interpreting something positively. This 'interpretation exercise' can also be carried out in pairs, with the positive interpretation of seemingly negative events being carried out together.

80 Three Times a Day: I Trust in Myself

People who have little self-assurance tend to be more programmed for failure. They tell themselves, 'I won't be able to do it anyway …', 'I don't think this will work out.', and then these statements tend to become self-fulfilling prophecies, because it is not only important that we try hard – we also have to believe that we can succeed. Therefore we need to learn to programme ourselves positively.

Positive thinking can strengthen us considerably. In order to achieve lasting success with this, the following exercise has to be carried out regularly, three times daily for at least four weeks. We programme ourselves positively by telling ourselves: 'I have hidden possibilities at my disposal. I have a lot of strength. That's why I can trust in myself and my abilities.'

By doing this, most people will experience increased self-confidence. Of course, there will always be the occasional setback; that is perfectly normal. What is important is that we continue to encourage ourselves: 'I can do this.'

Who has already had experiences with positive thinking? What do they want to tell the group about this?

81 Stop-Signals

Developing self-confidence requires encouragement and support. We can also give ourselves this support. Every time we notice that we are having doubts in ourselves, that our thoughts are making out problems that probably are not even there, we should tell ourselves very consciously and clearly: 'Stop! I am thinking positively! I believe in myself! I can do this! I will think about and consider everything that could happen tonight.'

The 'stop-signal' can be repeated as often as doubts recur. When it has been well practised it does actually help to stop fears and worries. And often, come the evening, we have forgotten what we were going to think about. We can also support each other using 'stop-signals'. When we notice that a group member is becoming overwhelmed by doubts about themselves, we can clearly counter these with a 'stop-signal'. Children's groups can also make an actual 'stop-signal', which is produced when necessary.

82 Visualising

Visualising is the conscious and active use of our fantasy and power of imagination in order to achieve goals, to overcome hurdles, and to foster our self-esteem. When we direct a visualisation at concrete behaviour this can support our activities and what we want to achieve under the motto: 'If you can picture yourself doing something then you can do it!'

In a group, members can be shown how they can use their imagination for support rather than for reinforcing their fear. Group members are asked to do a particular task: for example, following an obstacle course with their eyes closed. Before the exercise actually starts, they can practise how they are going to manage the task. First, they do the task with their eyes open. They walk the course, remember the obstacles, the path between them and the calls. Then, in their imagination, they do the task again with their eyes closed. They imagine the course and the goal as concretely as possible. They listen with their inner ear for the calls that tell them whether they have to manoeuvre to the left or right of an obstacle, until they have reached their goal – without knocking down a single obstacle. They repeat this visualisation until the task and the course are totally clear and familiar in their mind. Then they actually do the obstacle course and let themselves be guided by the calls of the other group members.

How did group members experience this exercise? Did the visualisation help them? Or did they nevertheless doubt themselves? What would they need to do differently or better in another visualisation?

83 Self-importance

Generally, we get used to being told off or punished for doing something wrong right from the very beginning. Then, when we grow up, we often punish ourselves. However, in order to strengthen our self-confidence, it makes much more sense to praise and reinforce ourselves when we have done something well, or have managed a difficult task. Praise and reinforcement motivate us to try the successful behaviour again, or to do something even better. Not all praise and reinforcement are equally suitable, though; they have to be appropriate. In other words, there is no need for a hymn of praise for relatively straightforward behaviour; they also have to be perceived by us as positive and pleasant. For example, self-confidence is hardly strengthened if we reward a young girl on a diet who has done well in her maths test with a large vanilla ice-cream with extra cream. Reinforcers should have more of a non-material than a material value.

In fact, the group can put together a list of appropriate 'reinforcers' for forthcoming 'reward-cases'. To do this, they form sub-groups of three to four people. Every person initially writes down for themselves three 'reinforcers' that they would enjoy with the group. For example:

Scott	Henry	Michelle
1 A barbecue	1 Playing Monopoly	1 A barbecue
2 A visit to the zoo	2 A barbecue	2 Going clubbing
3 An extra PE lesson	3 Playing chess	3 Inviting a band

Next each sub-group exchanges wishes. They may already be finding 'common' reinforcers when doing this: for example, a barbecue. In any case, each sub-group agrees on at least three common reinforcers. Those are then brought to the whole group. Together, at least three reinforcers are identified that are good for everybody. They are written down as a list and kept somewhere safe. The list can be referred to whenever praise for special strength is called for.

Also, every group member can, for themselves, put together a personal 'collection of reinforcers' and reinforce themselves for 'strong' behaviour. Unfortunately, there is not always someone there who looks after them. In that case, self-importance is expressly allowed!

Self-obligations

A good way of supporting oneself in the realisation of good intentions is a contract that one agrees with oneself. Such a contract could, for example, look like this:

CONTRACT

I _____(name) agree with myself that, by the _____(date), I will turn the following resolution into action: _____

_____

_____

_____

(Signature)

The following person is given a copy of this contract:

_____

(Name)

He/She will support me in keeping to this contract, will return the contract at the time agreed, and celebrate the completion of the contractually determined resolution.

_____

(Place and Date)

_____

(Signature)

It gives additional support if the contract is not simply put in a drawer, but a friend is asked to countersign the contract. Together, you can monitor whether the contract is kept, and celebrate the successful ending of its duration.

Together we are Strong

'Becoming strong' does not mean the selfish achievement of individual interests. Instead, it is about getting to know one's own desires, interests and needs, and to express them, and stand up for them, in a socially acceptable way. 'I-strong' behaviour does not only comprise self-directed abilities, but also socially-directed abilities, such as respect for others and empathy.

Appropriate self-assertion is an essential part of interaction and co-operation skills. Being self-confident and asserting oneself in social situations also involves behaving in such a way that, while one's own interests are maintained, interests of others are respected, too, and (where possible) are not restricted. All forms of aggressive assertion are excluded.

Instead of confrontation, co-operation is sought. Being able to manage tasks together, to support others, to be able to compromise, and to solve conflicts conjointly are essential behaviours of 'strong' personalities.

This section presents a compilation of games and exercises for the following topics:

◆ Getting involved with each other
◆ Treating each other with consideration and respect
◆ Supporting each other
◆ Managing tasks together
◆ And, from all this, gaining joint strength.

85 Back Pushing

That we are generally stronger when co-operating with others can be demonstrated with a simple exercise. The group is divided into two equally large sub-groups. Each sub-group forms a long line, shoulder to shoulder, arm in arm. The lines stand back-to-back opposite each other. A chalk line is drawn between the two sub-groups, or a natural line in the floor, such as the beginning of a carpet, is used.

When a signal is given, the two groups try to push each other across the line. Is it working? If so, could a different line-up of group members in the 'weaker' line provide more strength? The groups experiment with different line-ups. When are they stronger, when weaker? In which order do individuals have to stand next to each other so that the group is at its strongest? Is it possible for the groups to be equally strong, so that they cannot push each other away?

86) Blind Snake

Without practice, this game is suitable for from two to 10 people. Therefore, a larger group should initially be divided into appropriately sized sub-groups. Up to 10 people form a queue. Everybody puts their hands on the shoulders of the person in front of them and, except for the 'snake's head', closes their eyes. Using previously agreed signals (such as stamping their foot, tapping the next member's left or right hand on their shoulder once or twice), the snake's head – the first group member in the queue – communicates to the next member of the blind snake how to get around obstacles such as slopes and stairs. These signals have to be passed on backwards from one snake member to the next. The snake's journey should take approximately five minutes.

How well did the journey go? What feelings did being 'blind' trigger in different snake members, near the snake's head or at the snake's end? How 'strong' was the snake as a whole?

When there is a lot of trust within the group, and with increasing practice, the snake can become longer. How many members can manage to be 'strong together'?

87 Getting Up Together

Small groups of four to five people are formed. They are seated in a small circle and have to get up from their chairs and sit down again at the same time without talking to each other.

How well did the different groups manage this? How did group members communicate? Were there leader roles? How did they come out? Who took them on? Were all group members happy with their roles?

Gradually, the groups can be enlarged. In the end, the whole group is seated in a circle and everybody tries to stand up and sit down at the same time, without saying a word and without agreeing a leader beforehand.

How did group members feel during this exercise? Superior or inferior? Strong together or more unsure? Did they find out something new about themselves and others?

88) Stable Interplay

For this exercise, the group needs to consist of an even number of people. They form a circle and hold each other's hands tightly. For this they should stand quite close together, and have a stable base. Then they count: 'in, out, in, out, …'. At a signal, everybody who said 'in' leans inwards and everybody who said 'out' leans outwards. Both feet have to remain firmly on the ground. If this works well, and everybody leaned inwards and outwards at the same time, positions can be changed. Everybody who is 'in' now leans 'out', and vice versa. This moving to and fro can now take place evenly and rhythmically, without instructions being necessary. The stability of the group is maintained through the rhythmical interplay of the counter forces.

What experiences did group members have during this exercise? Was it difficult to get involved in it? How great was the trust in oneself and in others?

(89) Circle of Trust

All group members form a circle. They stand shoulder to shoulder, facing the middle. They reach their arms forward at chest height. Everybody has to have a stable base. To make sure they really stand firmly, they have to balance their weight in the standing position.

One group member volunteers to stand in the middle, crosses their arms in front of their chest, and closes their eyes. When everybody in the circle is standing firm, the volunteer lets themselves fall with a straight and relaxed body against the reaching-out hands of the others, moving forwards, backwards, to the side, as the group pushes them gently back.

Group members take it in turn to be in the middle. However, no one should be forced to take on this position. Group members have to decide for themselves: How much trust do I have in the others? How much trust do I have in myself, so that I can get involved in this situation? Afterwards, they ask themselves: What was my experience during this exercise? How do I feel now after the exercise?

(90) Balancing Pencils

The group is divided into pairs. Every pair is given a pencil. Together they now have to balance this pencil, using their right or left index fingers. While they are doing this, pairs move around freely in the room. They are not allowed to talk to each other and, of course, they are not allowed to drop the pencils. After a little while, instructions are given: move forwards, lift your arms, walk around, squat down, and so on.

How long does it take for the first pencil to fall? How long does the whole group manage to balance their pencils? The exercise can also be carried out using balloons that are balanced between heads – forehead to forehead.

How difficult was this exercise? How did the pairs communicate with each other? Who took on the lead, who was led? How did pairs communicate with other pairs?

91 **A Sky Full of Balloons**

The group requires as many balloons as there are group members. Everybody throws their balloons up in the air or at each other. The balloons have to be kept moving continuously; no balloon is allowed to fall to the floor.

How long did the group manage to keep the balloons going in the air? How much does the time increase as the group members manage to concentrate more on each other?

92 Chain Reaction

The group members spread out in the room. One group member starts the game by calling another group member who has something that is similar to themselves; for example, they also wear glasses, are wearing a blue shirt, and so on. The second group member holds on to the first group member and in turn calls a group member who has something in common with themselves. The game continues in this way until all group members are connected.

The game can be repeated as often as you like. The result is that a new sequence is produced every time, which makes for visible evidence that the group belongs together in many ways, and that differences between members are actually only relative.

Did individuals know before this how many similarities there were between them?

Strong Triplets

The group is divided into groups of three. (So that everybody can participate, one or two groups of four can also be formed, with the instructions being amended accordingly.) Each group has to work on the following tasks. They have to name:

◆ Three weaknesses that all three group members reject: for example, lying, not being able to fight back, blushing

◆ Three strengths that all three of them have or would like to have: for example, voicing their own opinion, being popular, getting lots of pocket money

◆ One weakness that only one of the group members has (or admits to), for example:
group member 1 does not dare to contradict anybody
group member 2 is not very good with money
group member 3 never finishes anything they have started

◆ A strength that only one of the group members has, for example:
group member 1 is good at judo
group member 2 is good with numbers
group member 3 stands up for weaker members.

The results from the sub-groups are then discussed by the whole group. Was it difficult to agree what were strengths and what were weaknesses? Was it difficult to talk about one's own strengths and weaknesses? Was it easy or difficult to find commonalities and differences? How many weaknesses and, more importantly, how many strengths are there in all the groups? Did group members find out something about others that they did not know?

(94) Shipwrecked

The group imagines that they are on a ship that has hit a rock near an uninhabited island. The ship is holed and is sinking gradually. Everybody has to get into the lifeboats. In order to ensure that they are going to make it to the uninhabited island, they can only take 10 items with them. In addition, they have to make sure they are going to take things that will safeguard their survival on the island. Initially, every group member makes an individual choice of 10 items they definitely want to take. Then they form groups of five. Each group has to agree on 10 things to take from all the things that the individuals wanted to take. The small groups continue to enlarge until the whole group is together again. Every time the group enlarges, luggage has to be sorted through, because in each group phase only 10 items can be taken.

What 10 items did the whole group agree on in the end? How difficult was it to agree on so few items? What criteria were used to choose items? Is everybody happy with the end result?

95 Encounter on a Narrow Bridge

A rope placed on the floor, or a footbridge marked out with chalk serves as a bridge. Two group members at a time encounter each other on the 'bridge'. The bridge is really very narrow. Anyone who stumbles falls into the river will drown. Therefore, the two members who meet really have to pass each other very carefully indeed. This only works with a lot a mutual help and consultation.

How did different group members solve this problem? How did they try to get past each other (holding on to each other, moving backwards, verbal and non-verbal arrangements, and so on)? How did they feel during this?

96 Ice Floe

The group divides into sub-groups of equal number. Each of these sub-groups goes and stands on an 'ice floe' (such as a piece of newspaper). The ice floe is threatening to melt. The group can prevent the ice floe melting by marking off as big a piece as possible with their feet. One group member marks off with a pen how much room the group needs. The better the group agrees how to position their feet, the more able the ice floe is to take their weight.

How difficult was the exercise? How difficult was the consultation? What did it feel like to have 'managed' the exercise reasonably well?

97 Co-operative Marathon

Many years ago the original marathon runners put a lot of effort into delivering messages over long distances that could not be managed by a single person. Therefore, each runner ran a certain distance, and messages were passed from runner to runner.

The task during this co-operative marathon is simply to cover a certain distance, or to cover a certain distance in a certain time. The distance that needs to be covered by each group member is adjusted according to their individual abilities. The distance and the time within which the distance is to be covered are given. Each group member has to participate. The group can now experiment to find how best to utilise everybody. Can the result be improved on?

Would it actually have been possible for one person to manage this exercise? How much time would they have needed? Was it difficult to utilise group members appropriately? Is it more tedious or less strenuous to manage a task together?

98 Five Against One

Using a chance principle, a small group of five people is formed. They imagine that one of their members is being approached by five threatening-looking attackers. What can a small group that is one member less do together against the attackers? They are given five minutes to come up with at least three creative and 'strong' solutions (that is, not hitting and not doing nothing). Such solutions could be:

◆ To shout 'fire' and point to somewhere behind the attackers
◆ To sink to their knees and start praying
◆ To imitate a dog barking.

Solutions can also be presented using role-play.

Afterwards, a new group is formed that has to think of further solutions to the attack.

This method can also be used to develop unusual, new solutions to other questions or concrete problems of the group. For example, the teacher favours the girls. He always gives them preferential treatment. Possible solutions are:

◆ Everybody has a tick list to record how often they put their arms up and how many times they were chosen
◆ The teacher consciously calls alternately a girl, a boy, a girl, and so on

◆ It is not the teacher who calls the next pupil; instead, the pupils form an answering chain. The pupil whose turn it was calls the next pupil.

In the end, the group agrees on one of the solutions and tries it out. After a certain amount of time, its effectiveness is evaluated; where necessary, the solution is changed, another solution is tried, and so on.

What are the experiences of the group when solving problems together? Did the group members know already that they could be this strong together?

99 Listening Collage: That's Us

For this exercise, the group requires a tape recorder with a microphone for recording. For the actual task, group members form small groups. Within the groups, they come up with 'strong' statements that they would like to tell about themselves. For example: 'We are the greatest.'; 'We don't fear anything or anybody.'; 'Whoever takes on one of us has to deal with all of us.'; or songs such as 'We are the Champions.'; or short dialogues, and so on. Ideas are then brought together in the whole group. Together, the 'manuscript' for the listening collage is compiled. What is supposed to be recorded? In what order? Who is going to talk, and who is going to sing?

When the contents and performers have been decided on, the group divides into the 'production groups' again for recording. Afterwards, the group works could be compiled into a joint listening collage on one tape, by recording from one tape recorder on to another (if a second tape recorder is available).

Was it easy or difficult to agree on a joint content? What experiences did group members have during the production of the listening collage? What feelings are triggered when listening to the completed listening collage? What does it feel like to belong to such a 'strong' group?

(100) A Lot of Strong People

The different members in a group all have their strengths. To make this clear, the following competition can be carried out. The group gives an award and claps for individual 'strengths' related to given criteria and abilities, for example:

◆ Who can speak best on behalf of the group?
◆ Who is particularly good at solving conflicts?
◆ Who is particularly good at comforting others when something has gone wrong?

Obviously, when choosing the questions, special care must be taken to ensure that every group member 'wins'.

The ensuing discussion should focus on bringing out the fact that every person has special strengths, and that there are a lot more 'strong' abilities than we are normally aware of. Has the group had new experiences? Have group members found out something new and unexpected about themselves and others?

101 Five Questions

For this exercise, each group member requires 15 small pieces of paper on to which they write their first name. The group as a whole, or each group member for themselves, now thinks of five questions that have something to do with the group members' strengths. For example:

◆ Which group members are most helpful?
◆ Which group members make the best suggestions?
◆ Which group members especially ensure a good group climate?
◆ Which group members encourage others most?
◆ Which group members have a calming influence when there is a lot of excitement?
◆ Which group members work particularly constructively?
◆ Which group members are particularly good at settling conflicts?

Now the first question is given. Each group member takes three of their pieces of paper, and thinks about which three group members the question is particularly appropriate for. Everybody distributes their pieces of paper to the people chosen. Who got the most pieces of paper? Is there someone who did not get any pieces of paper? Why is that? The discussion needs to bring out the point that there cannot be any 'right' or 'wrong' allocations, but that, by distributing pieces of paper, subjective opinions only are expressed. The same procedure is carried out for the next four questions. Of course, not all questions need to reflect pedagogical seriousness; fun and humour should be included, for example, with a question such as: 'Who sweetens up the lives of the group members?'

(102) Mentors at Work

To make sure all members of a group can be strong, it is important that they support each other, and especially give strength to those whose self-confidence is not so well developed.

For a given amount of time (for younger children, one to two days, for older ones, several days, a week or a month), each group member becomes another member's 'mentor'. To do this, everybody writes their name on a piece of paper. Pieces of paper are shuffled and drawn anonymously. (The drawer's name is put back and another one taken out.) During 'mentor time', group members keep a particular eye on their secret friend; give them courage when they are showing signs of weakness, or do not dare to do something, and help them in a concrete, but non-imposing manner. For example, they address them specifically; choose them to be part of their group during groupwork time; encourage them to put their hand up; include them in discussions, and so on. When 'brownie time' is up, the whole group discusses their experiences during brownie time. (The respective mentor relationships can be, but do not have to be, revealed at this point.)

(103) Pictograms

Pictograms are signs of our time. The special thing about pictograms is that their meaning is so evidently clear that any additional explanation is superfluous. Everybody immediately knows what is meant. What pictograms does the group know?

The group now tries to design pictograms as symbols for a 'strong community'. They can work on their own, or in small groups.

The different pictograms are exhibited and looked at together. The most succinct are selected to symbolise the strong community. Pictograms can also provide motifs for 'buttons'.

(104) Making Up Co-operative Game Rules

The majority of games are aimed not at common grounds, but at winning and losing. Consequently, there always have to be 'weak' players. However, many of these games can also be played co-operatively and still be fun. The only condition is that the rules of the game have to be changed co-operatively.

Group members are asked to bring in their favourite games, or to explain their favourite games, and together new, co-operative rules are invented. For example:

◆ Dominoes – The aim of the game is not to put down as many pieces as possible, or to put down the last piece; instead, everybody puts their pieces together to create a particularly nice picture.

◆ Ludo – The aim of the game is no longer to arrive first with all your counters; instead, everybody tries to help each other, so that as many players as possible get their counter in at the same time; then the second one, the third, the fourth.

◆ A ball game where, usually, two teams try to hit an opponent with a soft ball, and thus put them out of the game. Here, pairs or triplets are formed, with a mix of weak and strong players. The aim is no longer to hit one person to put them out of the game, but to hit all the people in a pair or triplet in order to score a point.

You can try to change the rules of many different games. Which ones work particularly well? Which ones have to be worked on to maintain the fun of the game?

(105) Rotation Theatre

So-called 'rotation theatre' can be used to demonstrate how well a group is working as a team; how well group members are tuned into each other, or what they have learned together. Rotation theatre is a method for setting free creative forces.

For example, the group plays scenarios related to the topic 'Together we are strong'. Depending on the size of the group, small groups of three to four people are formed. One of the groups starts the play, either on a voluntary basis, or by luck of the draw. They get five minutes to think of a beginning related to the topic. While they are playing, the next group prepares their part. Everybody else watches the play. The play can continue as long as the individual groups feel like playing. Play scenarios are not compared or evaluated. There should be time at the end of the rotation theatre to exchange with each other experiences during the play and thoughts while watching the play.

(106) Powerful Puzzle

This exercise is particularly useful for reflecting on previous exercises related to strength and self-confidence, or for giving feedback. It can also be used to demonstrate how strong a group is when many people put their abilities together.

A piece of cardboard is cut into as many pieces as there are group members present. The pieces are well shuffled and everybody takes one piece. Everybody then writes a 'strong' sentence or draws a 'strong' picture on their piece. Afterwards, puzzle pieces are put together and then stuck together.

Finally, group members can look at the puzzle and discuss how 'strong' group members are as a team.

Designing Shop Windows

This exercise allows group members to experience the topic 'team work' in a creative way. It is also useful for reflection.

The group divides into sub-groups of five to eight people. These small groups take part in a 'shop window competition'. Each group has to design a shop window with the motto, 'Together we are strong'. The group members can design their shop window simply through facial expression and gesture. They can also use any materials that are available in the room or that have been brought in especially, such as items of clothing, single pieces of furniture, newspapers or books.

After completion, group members visit each other's 'shop windows', and (where possible) photos of shop windows are taken, using an instant or digital camera. Depending on the number of group members, the group can also form two sub-groups. One group designs the 'shop window', the other observes and evaluates. Then they swap roles.

(108) Together we are Strong

The group jointly tells a story about their 'being strong'. First, they agree a 'strong' title, such as: 'A strong community', or 'How, one day, we proved our strength'. Then the group invents a story in which each group member features with a positive 'strong' characteristic, behaviour, ability and so on.

To do this, the group is seated in a circle. Each group member has to make up a sentence in which they mention positively the person on their right. A group member volunteers to start, or someone is selected using random selection. When they have finished their sentence they pass on the word to the left.

How difficult was it to say something strong about everybody and, at the same time, come up with a completed story? Was the first story immediately successful, or did the group require another go?

Solving Conflicts Together

From time to time, there will be conflicts in any group. A 'strong' group is able to handle these together and in a constructive manner. Resolving conflicts is not a matter of winning and losing. Those involved in the conflict should find a solution that they can all live with.

All group members are seated in a circle. Those involved in the conflict choose from among themselves one or two representatives they trust. These lead the conflict discussion and try for a settlement. The conflict discussion follows the following procedure. The facts are explained. One after the other, those involved report, without being interrupted, how they experienced the conflict. The part individual people had in the conflict is worked out. To do this, the following questions are useful:

◆ What were those involved trying to achieve?
◆ What did they say and/or do?

Solutions are suggested and agreed – preferably by those involved. Agreements are put down in writing.

The main part of working towards resolving the conflict is carried out by those immediately involved in the conflict and their representatives. If they are unable to find solutions, the remaining group members can also make suggestions or be approached for advice. In any case, the group can be jointly responsible for ensuring that agreements decided upon are observed.

How difficult is it to resolve conflicts in this way, jointly and in public? Are there certain conflict topics that keep recurring within the group? Are there particular group members who are always involved in conflicts? In such cases, what can the group do to prevent conflicts in the first place?

(**110**) Sharing Tasks

All tasks and duties that come up within the group (watering plants, sweeping the room, getting drinks, fetching keys, looking after the group's kitty, and so on) are written down on index cards. On the cards is also noted down how many people can carry out a particular task together. All together, there need to be as many responsibilities as there are group members.

The cards are then laid out openly. Every group member has to put themselves down for something by writing their names on the relevant cards, even when they do not like the task that is the only one left. In such a case, they can try to swap once all tasks have been covered. However, this is only possible under mutual agreement and on a voluntary basis. At the same time as sharing out the tasks, group members can also practise formulating requests, turning down demands, and coping with rejection. The tasks are only shared out for a certain period – say for a week or a month – depending on how often the group meets. Then they are shared out anew.

To make choosing tasks fairer, group members can agree on an order of choice that changes every time, so that, eventually, everybody will have the opportunity to have first choice of the tasks available.

How strong is the 'community'? How self-confident are group members when dealing with each other? What are their feelings while tasks are shared out?

(111) Having Gained Strength

At the end of a course, a working party, a (school) year, the holidays and so on, group members pack their rucksacks or suitcases. They put in everything they have gained in strength together and that they want to take home for themselves. If the group or class is going to continue, the 'luggage' can be taken to new group sessions or lessons and be unpacked again: that's how strong we are already!

◆ **happiness**
◆ **friendship**
◆ **more self-confidence**